D0786580

THE NATIONAL COUNTERTERRORISM CENTER

Series Titles

CITIZEN SOLDIERS: THE NATIONAL GUARD

CUSTOMS AND BORDER PROTECTION

DEFENDING THE SKIES: THE AIR FORCE

DEFENDING THE GROUND: THE ARMY

DEFENDING THE SEAS: THE NAVY

THE DRUG ENFORCEMENT ADMINISTRATION

HOMELAND SECURITY

THE NATIONAL COUNTERTERRORISM CENTER

PROTECTING AGAINST BIOLOGICAL AND CHEMICAL ATTACK

PUTTING OUT FIRES: FIREFIGHTERS

RESCUING HOSTAGES: THE FBI

STOPPING CRIME: THE POLICE

Defending Our Nation

The National Counterterrorism Center

FOREWORD BY
MANNY GOMEZ, ESQ., SECURITY AND TERRORISM EXPERT

BY
KELLY KAGAMAS TOMKIES

MASON CREST

Mason Crest
450 Parkway Drive, Suite D
Broomall, PA 19008
www.masoncrest.com

Printed in the United States of America
First printing
9 8 7 6 5 4 3 2 1

Series ISBN: 978-1-4222-3759-5
Hardcover ISBN: 978-1-4222-3766-3
ebook ISBN: 978-1-4222-8022-5

Library of Congress Cataloging-in-Publication Data

Names: Tomkies, Kelly Kagamas, author.
Title: The National Counterterrorism Center / foreword by Manny Gomez, Esq.,
  Security and Terrorism Expert ; by Kelly Kagamas Tomkies.
Description: Broomall, Pa. : Mason Crest, [2018] | Series: Defending our nation | Includes index.
Identifiers: LCCN 2016053112| ISBN 9781422237663 (hardback) | ISBN
  9781422237595 (series) | ISBN 9781422280225 (ebook)
Subjects: LCSH: National Counterterrorism Center (U.S.)--Juvenile literature.
  | Terrorism--United States--Prevention--Juvenile literature.
Classification: LCC HV6432 .T655 2018 | DDC 363.325/170973--dc23
LC record available at https://lccn.loc.gov/2016053112

Developed and Produced by Print Matters Productions, Inc.
(www.printmattersinc.com)

Cover and Interior Design by Bill Madrid, Madrid Design

CONTENTS

FOREWORD BY MANNY GOMEZ, ESQ. 6

1 HISTORY OF COUNTERTERRORISM 8

2 THE NCTC'S ORGANIZATION 16

3 ASSESSING THREATS AT THE NCTC.......... 26

4 WORKING FOR THE NCTC.................... 42

5 TECHNOLOGY DRIVEN 52

6 JCAT 62

SERIES GLOSSARY 71

CHRONOLOGY....................................... 74

FURTHER RESOURCES 76

INDEX 77

ABOUT THE AUTHOR AND PICTURE CREDITS 80

KEY ICONS TO LOOK FOR:

Words to understand: These words with their easy-to-understand definitions will increase the reader's understanding of the text while building vocabulary skills.

Sidebars: This boxed material within the main text allows readers to build knowledge, gain insights, explore possibilities, and broaden their perspectives by weaving together additional information to provide realistic and holistic perspectives.

Educational Videos: Readers can view videos by scanning our QR codes, providing them with additional educational content to supplement the text. Examples include news coverage, moments in history, speeches, iconic sports moments and much more!

Text-dependent questions: These questions send the reader back to the text for more careful attention to the evidence presented there.

Research projects: Readers are pointed toward areas of further inquiry connected to each chapter. Suggestions are provided for projects that encourage deeper research and analysis.

Series glossary of key terms: This back-of-the book glossary contains terminology used throughout this series. Words found here increase the reader's ability to read and comprehend higher-level books and articles in this field.

FOREWORD

VIGILANCE

We live in a world where we have to have a constant state of awareness—about our surroundings and who is around us. Law enforcement and the intelligence community cannot predict or stop the next terrorist attack alone. They need the citizenry of America, of the world, to act as a force multiplier in order to help deter, detect, and ultimately defeat a terrorist attack.

Technology is ever evolving and is a great weapon in the fight against terrorism. We have facial recognition, we have technology that is able to detect electronic communications through algorithms that may be related to terrorist activity—we also have drones that could spy on communities and bomb them without them ever knowing that a drone was there and with no cost of life to us.

But ultimately it's human intelligence and inside information that will help defeat a potential attack. It's people being aware of what's going on around them: if a family member, neighbor, coworker has suddenly changed in a manner where he or she is suddenly spouting violent anti-Western rhetoric or radical Islamic fundamentalism, those who notice it have a duty to report it to authorities so that they can do a proper investigation.

In turn, the trend since 9/11 has been for international communication as well as federal and local communication. Gone are the days when law enforcement or intelligence organizations kept information to themselves and didn't dare share it for fear that it might compromise the integrity of the information or for fear that the other organization would get equal credit. So the NYPD wouldn't tell anything to the FBI, the FBI wouldn't tell the CIA, and the CIA wouldn't tell the British counterintelligence agency, MI6, as an example. Improved as things are, we could do better.

We also have to improve global propaganda. Instead of dropping bombs, drop education on individuals who are even considering joining ISIS. Education is salvation. We have the greatest production means in the world through Hollywood and so on, so why don't we match ISIS materials? We tried it once but the government itself tried to produce it. This is something that should definitely be privatized. We also need to match the energy of cyber attackers—and we need savvy youth for that.

There are numerous ways that you could help in the fight against terror—joining law enforcement, the military, or not-for-profit organizations like the Peace Corps. If making the world a safer place appeals to you, draw on your particular strengths and put them to use where they are needed. But everybody should serve and be part of this global fight against terrorism in some small way. Certainly, everybody should be a part of the fight by simply being aware of their surroundings and knowing when something is not right and acting on that sense. In the investigation after most successful attacks, we know that somebody or some persons or people knew that there was something wrong with the person or persons who perpetrated the attack. Although it feels awkward to tell the authorities that you believe somebody is acting suspicious and may be a terrorist sympathizer or even a terrorist, we have a higher duty not only to society as a whole but to our family, friends, and ultimately ourselves to do something to ultimately stop the next attack.

It's not *if* there is going to be another attack, but where, when, and how. So being vigilant and being proactive are the orders of the day.

Manny Gomez, Esq.
President of MG Security Services,
Chairman of the National Law Enforcement Association,
former FBI Special Agent, U.S. Marine, and NYPD Sergeant

CHAPTER 1

HISTORY OF COUNTER-TERRORISM

U.S. President Franklin Delano Roosevelt, creator of the U.S. intelligence apparatus, shown in 1940.

Today's National Counterterrorism Center formed after September 11, 2001, to protect America's security in times of crisis. Part of the Intelligence Reform and Terrorism Prevention Act of 2004, the NCTC is staffed by personnel from multiple departments and agencies from across the intelligence community. NCTC is organizationally part of the Office of the Director of National Intelligence (ODNI).

Prior to the formation of the NCTC, the Central Intelligence Agency (CIA) was responsible for gathering all intelligence for the government, including counterterrorism intelligence. So NCTC's history begins with the formation of the CIA. The U.S. government has always collected secret information for national security purposes. Before World War II, those files reached the White House from the Department of State, the Federal Bureau of Investigation (FBI), and various special military units. These organizations, however, competed with one another instead of sharing their information. This departmental jealousy had to end when Adolf Hitler's Nazi regime waged war in Europe in the late 1930s. President Franklin D. Roosevelt created the Office of Coordinator of Information (COI) on July 11, 1941, and this agency later became the model for the CIA. Its first head, Major General William J. Donovan, is still called "the godfather of the CIA."

Donovan was known as Wild Bill because he had a dynamic character and loved action. This energy was certainly needed to organize the COI and ensure that it survived. When America entered World War II after the Japanese attacked Pearl Harbor on December 7, 1941, the Joint Chiefs of Staff wanted to break up the COI. Donovan, however, kept his organization

Words to Understand

Guerrilla campaigns: Battles fought by independent soldiers not part of a specific group.

Counterintelligence: Activity meant to hide truth or protect a secret from an enemy.

Covert operations: Secret plans and activities carried out by spies and their agencies.

An aerial view of the Central Intelligence Agency headquarters, Langley, VA.

together, operating independently, but reporting to the Joint Chiefs of Staff. On June 13, 1942, the COI became the Office of Strategic Services (OSS).

By late 1944, the OSS had nearly 13,000 employees, and some people joked that OSS stood for "Oh So Social" because it hired so many distinguished people. Its agents used devices of a type now associated with James Bond, such as cameras disguised as matchboxes, messages in hollowed-out silver dollars, and coat buttons holding a compass inside. The OSS also joined with Britain's Special Operations Executive (SOE) to fight **guerrilla campaigns** in Europe and Asia.

After the Allied victory, the U.S. government disbanded the OSS on October 1, 1945. However, two branches were saved—Secret Intelligence, which dealt with foreign intelligence; and X-2, whose task was **counterintelligence**. In January 1946, President Harry S. Truman combined them to form the Central Intelligence Group (CIG). The National Security Act of 1947 turned the CIG into the independent CIA, no longer under the Joint Chiefs of Staff.

The first CIA director was Rear Admiral Roscoe H. Hillenkoetter. He had an easier job than "Wild Bill" Donovan, because many of the employees had already been trained by the OSS. The agency now had

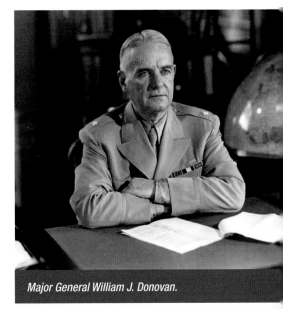

Major General William J. Donovan.

The Office of the Director of National Intelligence and National Counterterrorism Center.

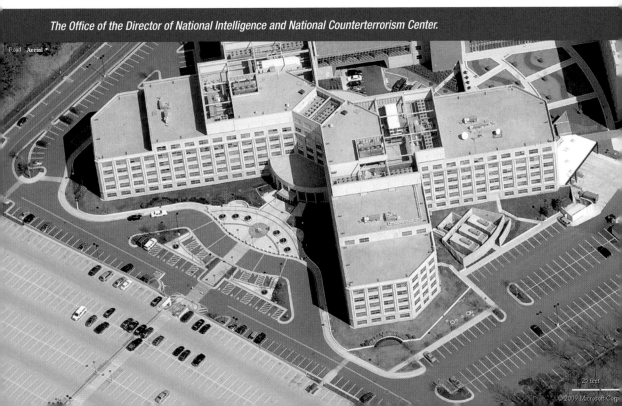

Road Aerial

25 feet

© 2009 Microsoft Corp

General William J. Donovan reviews Operational Group members in Bethesda, MD, prior to their departure for China in 1945.

to help contain **Communism** during the **Cold War** with the Soviet Union. The CIA looked for "the enemy within" the United States, and its overseas agents undertook dangerous **covert operations** to gather information, conducting a "war of spies" with Soviet agents of the KGB. America's first real battle against Communist forces was the Korean War (1950–1953), when the CIA gathered military information using Korean and Chinese agents.

Learn how early intelligence operatives survived in the field.

The Spy with a Limp

The woman who retired from the CIA in 1966 could have been anyone's favorite grandmother. She was, in fact, one of history's most successful agents. Born in Baltimore, Virginia Hall studied languages and worked in the U.S. embassy in Warsaw, Poland.

Despite losing her left leg after a hunting accident, she joined the British Special Operations Executive during World War II and was sent to France to establish a spy network in Vichy. This she managed, also helping prisoners of war to escape. Pursued by the Nazis, she escaped by foot over the Pyrenees Mountains to Spain.

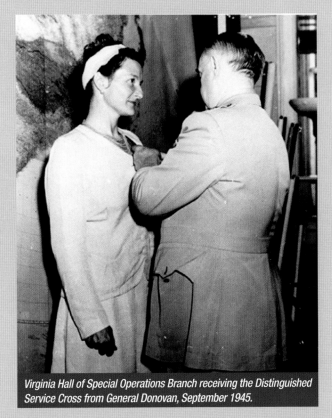

Virginia Hall of Special Operations Branch receiving the Distinguished Service Cross from General Donovan, September 1945.

Virginia then joined "Wild Bill" Donovan's Office of Strategic Services as a radio operator and returned to France. Told that the Nazi's brutal secret police force, the Gestapo, was determined to find the "woman with the limp," she taught herself to walk without one. At night, she trained and led French resistance forces in guerrilla warfare and sabotage, coordinating air-drops for the D-Day invasion of France on June 6, 1944.

In 1945, Virginia became the only woman civilian to be awarded America's Distinguished Service Cross. After the war, she became one of the CIA's first female operations officers, serving her country for another two decades.

A U-2 reconnaissance photograph of Cuba, showing Soviet nuclear missiles, their transports and tents for fueling and maintenance.

The 1960s began badly. The Russians shot down the CIA's U2 spy plane in 1960, and the next year, the agency was blamed for the Bay of Pigs failure, when it encouraged Cuban exiles in the United States to invade Communist Cuba. However, the CIA proved its worth in 1962, when a U2 flight discovered the Soviet missile buildup in Cuba, and President John F. Kennedy forced their removal. By the late 1960s, however, the agency had again lost the confidence of many Americans, who were protesting against the Vietnam War and questioning their government's role in the affairs of other nations.

Americans nevertheless turned again to the CIA in the 1980s to meet the rise of international terrorism. With the collapse of Communism in the 1990s, the agency could concentrate on finding hidden networks of terrorists. After the horrific attacks on America on September 11, 2001, the CIA quickly joined with the FBI and other organizations to lead the nation's counterterrorism efforts. Then, with the Intelligence Reform and Terrorism Prevention Act of 2004 (IRTPA), the NCTC formed. The NCTC's mission was to lead the nation's effort to combat terrorism at home and abroad by analyzing the threat, sharing that information with the organization's partners, and integrating all instruments of national power to ensure unity of effort.

Text-Dependent Questions

1. Which government agencies collected information for national security purposes before the formation of the CIA?
2. Why was William J. Donovan known as Wild Bill?
3. Which two branches of the former OSS were combined to form the CIA?

Research Projects

1. Research the CIA's role during the Bay of Pigs situation during President Kennedy's term of office. What vital information did the agency provide? How were they able to obtain it?
2. Learn more about the KGB. Did it form before or after the CIA? How many agents did it have? How often did the two agencies interact?

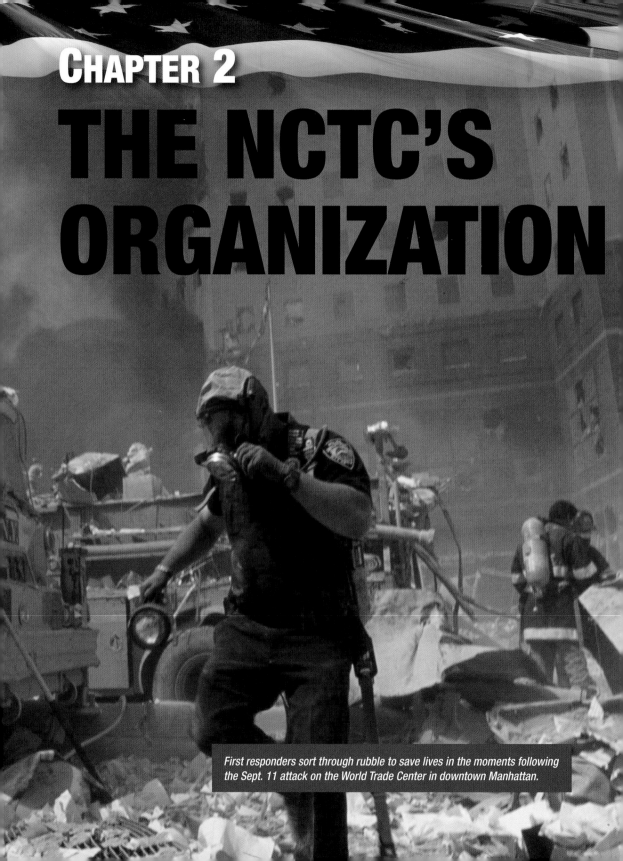

CHAPTER 2
THE NCTC'S ORGANIZATION

First responders sort through rubble to save lives in the moments following the Sept. 11 attack on the World Trade Center in downtown Manhattan.

The National Counterterrorism Center (NCTC) is the most unique governmental organization in the country. It is a conglomeration of the efforts of several agencies, including the FBI and CIA. Its director reports directly to the president, and to the Director of National Intelligence.

As of 2014, the director of the NCTC is Nicholas "Nick" Rasmussen. Rasmussen was sworn in on December 18, 2014, after being confirmed by the U.S. Senate. Previously, he served as deputy director of the organization and held a senior policy and planning position with the NCTC for three years prior to that. Rasmussen has taught a course on counterterrorism at Georgetown University.

The heart of the NCTC organization is the Joint Counterterrorism Assessment Team (JCAT). This team receives notification of any terrorist threats and assesses them to determine their credibility and likelihood. But not all JCAT members work in one central location. In fact most are members of other organizations and have been trained to serve joint duty—with their home organizations and the NCTC. According to NCTC, JCAT members are state, local, tribal, and territorial first responders and public safety professionals from around the country, working side by side with federal intelligence analysts from the NCTC, the Department of Homeland Security (DHS), and the Federal Bureau of Investigation (FBI) to research, produce, and **disseminate** counterterrorism intelligence.

Words to Understand

Disseminate: Disperse throughout.

Domestic: Relating to or originating in a country, especially one's own country.

Interagency: Between or among agencies.

In addition, the NCTC works with a long list of what it calls key partners, organizations whose missions are broader than counterterrorism but who have a big stake in combating terrorism:

- Central Intelligence Agency
- Defense Intelligence Agency
- Department of Agriculture
- Department of Defense
- Department of Energy
- Department of Health and Human Services
- Department of Homeland Security
- Department of Justice
- Department of State
- Department of the Treasury
- Drug Enforcement Administration
- Federal Bureau of Investigation
- National Geospatial Intelligence Agency
- Nuclear Regulatory Commission
- National Security Agency
- Transportation Security Administration
- U.S. Capitol Police

Hear from the director of the nation's nerve center for defending against terrorism.

Terrorist Attacks

In recent years, Americans have been subjected to many terrorist attacks, even before the tragic events of September 11, 2001. The most infamous assaults include the following:

- October 23, 1983: A suicide bomber blows up Marine headquarters in Beirut, Lebanon, killing 241 Marines and Navy personnel.

A view of the damage to the U.S. Embassy after the 1983 Beirut bombing.

- December 21, 1988: Libyans bomb Pan American Flight 103 over Lockerbie, Scotland, killing 270 people.

The wrecked cockpit of Pan Am Flight 103 with visible painted lettering reading, "Clipper Maid of the Seas.

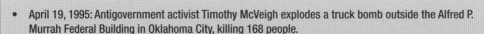

- April 19, 1995: Antigovernment activist Timothy McVeigh explodes a truck bomb outside the Alfred P. Murrah Federal Building in Oklahoma City, killing 168 people.
- August 7, 1998: U.S. embassies are bombed in Nairobi, Kenya, killing 291 people; and in Dar es Salaam, Tanzania, killing 10.
- October 12, 2000: A small ship carrying explosives rams the USS *Cole* off the coast of Yemen, killing 17 sailors.

The USS Cole *is towed away from the port city of Aden, Yemen, after the attack.*

The MV Blue Marlin *carrying the damaged* USS Cole.

The USS Cole after the Al Qaeda suicide attack.

- September 11, 2001: Islamic terrorists hijack four airliners, crashing two of them into the twin towers of the World Trade Center in New York City, killing more than 2,800 people and destroying both skyscrapers. A third hits the Pentagon, causing 189 deaths, and a fourth crashes into the Pennsylvania countryside, killing all 45 on board, after passengers overpower the hijackers.

The north face of Two World Trade Center (south tower) immediately after being struck by United Airlines Flight 175.

The remains of 6, 7, and 1 WTC on September 17, 2001

- December 2, 2015: A husband-and-wife team murder 14 and wound 22 others in San Bernardino, CA. The wife, a Pakistani national, was thought to have radicalized her husband, a U.S. citizen, who gunned down his parks department coworkers in the name of ISIS.
- June 13, 2016: A lone gunman opens fire in a gay nightclub in Orlando, FL. He kills 49 people, and 53 people are injured during the attack. The gunman, Omar Mateen, age 29, pledged alliance to ISIL.

NCTC's somewhat daunting tasks include the following:

- Integrating and analyzing all intelligence pertaining to terrorism possessed or acquired by the U.S. government (except purely domestic terrorism)
- Serving as the central and shared knowledge bank on terrorism information
- Ensuring that agencies receive all-source intelligence support needed to execute their counterterrorism plans or to perform independent, alternative analysis, and receive the intelligence needed to accomplish their assigned activities

Airport security stations at Seattle–Tacoma International Airport.

NCTC's Most Wanted

Each year the NCTC publishes a calendar that provides detailed information about the state of terrorism in the United States and abroad. It includes the names and descriptions of the terrorist organizations that are among the most dangerous and active in the world, as well as their leaders and other members who are considered dangerous and active. Here are the top five most wanted terrorists, according to the NCTC:

Abu Bakr al-Baghdadi, leader of the Islamic State of Iraq and the Levant (ISIL)

Ayman al-Zawahiri, leader of Al Qaeda

Mugshot of Abu Bakr al-Baghdadi taken by U.S. armed forces while in detention at Camp Bucca in the vicinity of Umm Qasr, Iraq, in 2004.

Dr. Ayman al-Zawahri in an image taken by Hamid Mir. Hamid Mir took this picture during his third and last interview with Osama bin Laden in November 2001 in Kabul. Dr.Ayman al-Zawahri was present in this interview and acted as the translator of Osama bin Laden.

Abu Du'a, also known as Abu Bakr al-Baghdadi, senior leader of ISIL
Abd al-Rahman Mustafa al-Qaduli, a senior member of ISIL
Abu Mohammed al-Adnani, born Taha Sobhi Falaha, official spokesman for and a senior leader of ISIL

Abu Mohammed al-Adnani, chief spokesperson for the Islamic State.

NCTC also serves as the principal adviser to the Director of National Intelligence on intelligence operations and analysis relating to counterterrorism. The organization advises the director on how well U.S. intelligence activities, programs, and budget proposals for counterterrorism conform to the priorities established by the president.

And unique among U.S. agencies, NCTC is the primary organization responsible for strategic operational planning for counterterrorism. Operating under the policy direction of the President and the National Security Council, NCTC provides **interagency** planning and assessments of U.S. strategic counterterrorism programs and activities.

When the NCTC receives a threat, the process is to assess that threat, and when appropriate, notify local NCTC partners to provide protection. The organization must also communicate to the general public any threats that may affect them.

Text-Dependent Questions

1. Who is the current head of the NCTC?
2. What is JCAT and what does it do?
3. What is the main responsibility of the organization?

Research Projects

1. Research how many people work for the NCTC both at the agency and jointly for local agencies. How many people are constantly on guard for terrorist threats?
2. Research to find out the average number of threats the NCTC receives each day. Then research to find out what percentage of those threats are transitioned into national alerts.

Chapter 3

Assessing Threats at the NCTC

A TSA security search.

According to a report published by the National Counterterrorism Center (NCTC), in 2010, the year for which data were analyzed, there were more than 11,500 terrorist attacks that occurred in 72 countries. Fortunately, says the NCTC, for about half of these attacks no loss of life occurred. Unfortunately, 13,200 people did die as a result of these attacks. How does the NCTC receive and assess terrorist threats? It is a process that takes multiagency and multidisciplinary cooperation.

Terrorist attacks are usually intended to influence opinions about governments and their politics. "International terrorism" is described as "terrorism involving the territory or the citizens of more than one country"—and in practice means that the person or group involved belongs to one nation and commits acts of terrorism in another nation. A "terrorist group" is any group that practices international terrorism. The job of the NCTC and other U.S. counterterrorist organizations is to anticipate and defend against such attacks within America and over-seas. The NCTC serves as a hub for all other military, law enforcement, and intelligence agencies' terrorist information. It is the only agency in the country in which all terrorist information is compiled and analyzed on a daily basis, in order for analysts to look for patterns where no other agency could see them.

Director of National Intelligence Dan Coats

Words to Understand

Cyberattack: An attack on computers through the use of the Internet.

Infrastructure: Foundation or basic structure.

Nonstate actors: Participants in an event who are unassociated with any government.

Radicalization: The process of becoming radical, or extreme, in political or religious views.

Discovering Terrorist Plans

There are a few ways that the NCTC can discover potential terrorist threats and plans. First, it can discover them "in house" utilizing its conglomeration of data compiled from law enforcement, military, FBI, and CIA data gathered all over the world. With access to the most complete information available, NCTC agents can often identify suspected terrorists and potential plans for attacks.

Another way the NCTC identifies threats is through tips from other government agencies and military branches. For example, the Transportation Security Administration (TSA) might detain someone at an airport and discover the potential for an attack. The TSA officer would alert the NCTC, whose agents would then comb their data to assess whether there was reason to believe the threat should be further investigated.

The TSA logo.

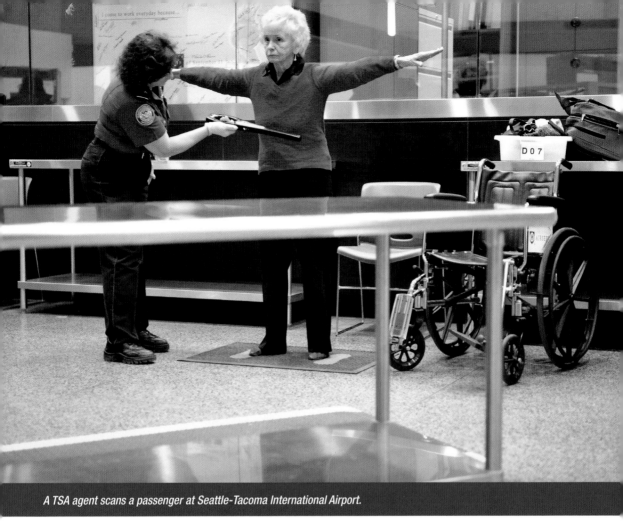

A TSA agent scans a passenger at Seattle-Tacoma International Airport.

The third primary way the NCTC could learn of a threat is through reporting by someone in the general public. Perhaps someone suspects a person in his or her neighborhood of compiling weapons or making bombs. This person then calls in to the NCTC and reports his or her suspicions. It is then up to the NCTC to determine whether these suspicions require further investigation.

While most people think of the traditional terrorist threats that involve violence, NCTC also assesses the threats of **cyberattacks**. In his February 2016 testimony to the U.S. Congress on terrorist threats to the United States, former Director of National Intelligence, James Clapper, said that cyber threats are becoming more concerning and may potentially become quite crippling to the U.S. and world economies and way of life.

The Coast Guard on counterterrorism patrol in Upper New York Bay.

Throughout the February worldwide threat assessment hearings, Clapper referred to the numerous threats facing the United States as a "litany of doom." Clapper said during his testimony that the United States is facing the most diverse global threat environment he has seen during his 55 years of government service. The threats range from violent extremists to infectious diseases to cyber criminals. In addition to the long-standing national security concerns of international terrorism and weapons of mass destruction, Clapper also addressed several emerging threats.

I want to briefly comment on both technology and cyber specifically. Technological innovation during the next few years will have an even more significant impact on our way of life. This innovation is central to our economic prosperity, but it will bring new security vulnerabilities," he said. "The Internet of things will connect tens of billions of new physical devices that could be exploited. Artificial intelligence will enable computers to make autonomous decisions about data and physical systems and potentially disrupt labor markets.

Cyberattacks by terrorists are likely, and their targets could be America's military, economic, telecommunications, or electrical systems. These are vital parts of the nation's **infrastructure**, and their destruction would halt practically all activity in America. Terrorists, for instance, could hack into Pentagon computers to steal secrets, or send viruses to crash the system, slowing or disrupting combat operations. The CIA has warned that the global expansion of information technology makes America more open to cyberattacks, and the NCTC is helping create ways to protect computer networks. In addition to cyberattacks, the Internet has become a place where terrorist organizations can recruit new members and the dark web a place where weapons and chemicals can be bought and sold. The NCTC monitors social media to track potential terrorist recruitment efforts, as well as monitoring communications between terrorists. Unfortunately, many terrorists are not using cell phones or the Internet to communicate anymore, to avoid intelligence gathering. Instant messaging systems in which the messages instantly disappear, such as iMessage, have become more prevalent, making monitoring nearly impossible.

NCTC also integrates foreign and domestic analysis from across the intelligence community (IC). The organization then uses these analyses to produce a wide range of detailed assessments designed to support senior policymakers and other members of the policy, intelligence, law enforcement, defense, homeland security, and foreign affairs communities. One example of an NCTC analytic product is the President's Daily Brief (PDB). As its name implies,

HOMELAND SECURITY ADVISORY SYSTEM

SEVERE
SEVERE RISK OF TERRORIST ATTACKS

HIGH
HIGH RISK OF TERRORIST ATTACKS

ELEVATED
SIGNIFICANT RISK OF TERRORIST ATTACKS

GUARDED
GENERAL RISK OF TERRORIST ATTACKS

LOW
LOW RISK OF TERRORIST ATTACKS

The original color-coded Homeland Secuirty Advisory System, which was replaced by the National Terrorism Advisory System in 2011.

the PDB updates the president of the United States on a daily basis on the state of terrorism and terrorist threats, both domestic and abroad. NCTC is also the central player in the Office of the Director of National Intelligence's (ODNI's)Homeland Threat Task Force (HTTF). HTTF orchestrates interagency collaboration and keeps senior policymakers informed about threats to the nation via a weekly update.

NCTC has formed specific groups to focus on specific threats. These groups use their expertise in these specific fields to provide expertise and analysis of key terrorism-related issues. The groups' work can have immediate and far-reaching impacts. For example, NCTC's Radicalization and Extremist Messaging Group leads the IC's efforts on radicalization issues. NCTC's Chemical, Biological, Radiological, Nuclear Counterterrorism Group brings together hard-to-find analytical, subject matter, and scientific expertise from NCTC and CIA on these critical issues.

NCTC also has the task of ensuring that all counterterrorist programs and efforts across the nation are of the highest quality. The organization evaluates the quality of counterterrorism analytic production, the training of analysts, and the strengths and weaknesses of the counterterrorism analytic workforce. NCTC created the Analytic Framework for Counterterrorism. The goal of the framework is to eliminate the redundancy of effort among counterterrorist agencies by delineating the roles of the IC's various counterterrorist analytic components.

Weapons of Mass Destruction

In the past, terrorists have tended to use bombs, but the intelligence community became increasingly concerned about the more dangerous threats posed by weapons of mass destruction (WMD), also known as CBRN—chemical, biological, radiological, and nuclear agents. Since the September 11 attacks, WMD have gained increased focus. The fear is that these methods can be used to poison the nation's food and water supply or even the air we breathe. It became clear that one agency needed to lead the efforts in protecting the country against this threat. In 2006, the FBI was chosen to be that agency. It created the WMD Directorate. This directorate has a workforce prepared to both prevent potential attacks and serve as first responders in the case of a successful attack.

Weapons of mass destruction symbols that are used worldwide.

Weapons of mass destruction response training.

One example of how the WMD Directorate has impacted national efforts in this area is the way it played a lead role in 2016 in training the nation's public safety bomb technicians.

Sharing Information

One of the NCTC's most important responsibilities is communication. The NCTC is by law the U.S. government's central and shared knowledge bank on known and suspected terrorists and international terror groups. NCTC provides all government agencies with the terrorism intelligence analysis and other information they need to fulfill their missions.

A meeting of the Biological Weapons Convention.

NCTC represents more than 30 intelligence, military, law enforcement, and homeland security networks under one roof, so that it can facilitate robust information sharing. NCTC was built to be a model of interagency information sharing, and it continues to serve in that capacity.

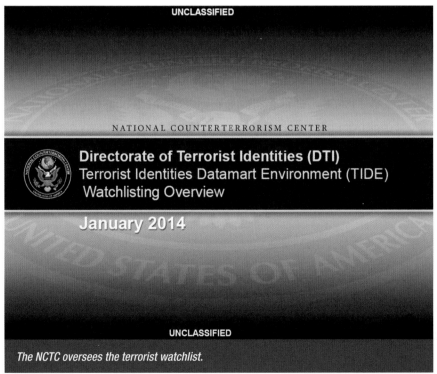

The NCTC oversees the terrorist watchlist.

The NCTC's consolidated repository of information on international terrorist identities is called the Terrorist Identities Datamart Environment (TIDE). TIDE provides the authoritative database that supports its Terrorist Screening Center as well as the U.S. government's watchlisting system. The center also produces NCTC Online (NOL) and NCTC Online CURRENT, classified websites that make counterterrorist products and articles available to users among approximately 75 government agencies, departments, military services, and major commands. Another important NCTC group is its Interagency Threat Assessment and Coordination Group (ITACG). ITACG facilitates information sharing between the IC and state, local, tribal, and private partners in coordination with the Department of Homeland Security (DHS), FBI, and other members of the ITACG Advisory Council.

NCTC is also tasked with providing the counterterrorist community with 24/7 situational awareness, terrorism threat reporting, and incident information tracking. To complete this task, NCTC hosts three daily secure video teleconferences (SVTC) and maintains constant voice and electronic contact with major intelligence and counterterrorism community players and foreign partners.

Integrating All Instruments of National Power

Here are more of the NCTC's organizational goals and duties:

- NCTC conducts strategic operational planning for counterterrorist activities across the U.S. government, integrating all instruments of national power, including diplomatic, financial, military, intelligence, homeland security, and law enforcement to ensure unity of effort.
- NCTC ensures effective integration of counterterrorist plans and synchronization of operations across more than 20 government departments and agencies engaged in the War on Terror, through a single and truly joint planning process.
- NCTC's planning efforts include broad, strategic plans such as the landmark National Implementation Plan (NIP) for the War on Terror.
- NCTC also prepares far more granular, targeted action plans to ensure integration, coordination, and synchronization on key issues, such as countering violent

extremism, terrorist use of the Internet, terrorist use of weapons of mass destruction, and counteroptions (after an attack).

- NCTC also leads interagency task forces designed to analyze, monitor, and disrupt potential terrorist attacks.
- NCTC assigns roles and responsibilities to departments and agencies as part of its strategic planning duties, but NCTC does not direct the execution of any resulting operations.
- NCTC monitors the alignment of all counterterrorism resources against the NIP and provides advice and recommendations to policy officials to enhance mission success.

The Oklahoma City Bomber

We tend to think that terrorists attacking American targets are foreigners. Most attacks that take place in the United States are, however, committed by U.S. citizens.

Before September 11, 2001, the most destructive terrorist attack in the United States had cost the lives of 168 people, including 19 children, and injured another 850, when a truck bomb destroyed the Alfred P. Murrah Federal Building in Oklahoma City on April 19, 1995.

Local police quickly caught the suspect, Timothy McVeigh. The investigation that followed, however, was headed by the FBI, the agency that handles terrorism within the United States. It formed an OKBOMB Task Force, and its 56 field offices helped collect evidence. The investigation was one of the most intense in the agency's history, involving more than 28,000 interviews, over 238,000 photographs, 23,290 items of evidence, and millions of pages of records. The agency's experts testified at the trial, linking McVeigh to the evidence. An FBI chemist found traces of an explosive on the man's clothing, and another FBI expert found his fingerprints on a receipt for bomb materials. McVeigh was found guilty on June 2, 1997, and executed on June 11, 2001. Terry Nichols, who assisted him, was sentenced to life.

The Oklahoma City bombing changed the way the FBI operates against terrorist groups. Before, it had to prove a particular federal crime had been, or was about to be, committed. Since this case, the FBI can act even if an extremist group is guilty only of discussing committing violent acts; such plans are discovered by operatives who have informants or who have themselves infiltrated terrorist organizations.

A view of the destroyed Alfred P. Murrah Federal Building, two days after the bombing.

Osama bin Laden and Beyond

"Dead or alive." That's the way President George W. Bush said that the United States wanted Osama bin Laden, one way or the other.

Bin Laden was born in 1957 in Saudi Arabia, the son of a billionaire. When his father died in 1986, he inherited about $80 million. In 1979, he went to Afghanistan to fight against the Soviet invasion. The United States supported the anti-Soviet forces, but the CIA has strongly denied rumors that it ever worked with, or even met, bin Laden. After the Soviets were defeated, bin Laden returned to Saudi Arabia to work in his family's construction business. He was now a hardened Islamic fundamentalist who believed that Muslims should live by the religion's strict centuries-old doctrines.

When the United States and its allies fought the Persian Gulf War in 1991 against Iraq to liberate Kuwait, bin Laden became angry that U.S. forces were stationed in Saudi Arabia. He called it "an occupation of the land of the holy places." His arguments with the Saudi monarchy forced him to move that year to Sudan, but five years later, its government responded to U.S. pressure and expelled him. Bin Laden then returned to Afghanistan, and in 1996, issued a fatwah, calling on Muslims to kill U.S. troops, justifying this order by referring to Islamic law. Two years later, he included all American civilians as potential targets.

Protected by Afghanistan's Taliban government, bin Laden created a large terrorist organization called Al Qaeda, which means "the base." He built training camps for his followers—estimated to number about 3,000 fighters—and began the series of bombings against U.S. targets, which led to the September 11 attacks that horrified the world. It also provoked a strong military response, which defeated the Taliban and scattered the Al Qaeda network. After months of gathering intelligence, a U.S. military operation on May 2, 2011, attacked bin Laden's compound in Abbottabad, Pakistan. During this raid bin Laden was killed.

As of 2016, the IC's primary person of interest is the leader of ISIL, Abu Bakr al-Baghdadi.

U.S. President Barack Obama (second from left) and Vice President Joe Biden (far left), along with national security personnel, receive an update on Operation Neptune's Spear, the mission that killed Osama bin Laden.

An aerial view of Osama bin Laden's compound in the Pakistani city of Abbottabad made by the CIA.

Text-Dependent Questions

1. What is international terrorism?
2. Name one method the NCTC uses to discover terrorists' plans.
3. What is the PDB and how is the NCTC involved in it?

Research Projects

1. Research the Interagency Threat Assessment and Coordination Group (ITACG). How active is the group and what is the complete list of agencies involved in it?
2. What is the scope of TIDE and how does NCTC protect the databases it houses?

CHAPTER 4

WORKING FOR THE NCTC

A U.S. Army technologist works with a Nigerian soldier to improve a translation program.

W ith the increased threat of many different kinds of terrorist attacks, there is a growing need for employees for a variety of jobs within the National Counterterrorism Center (NCTC). From administrators to watch officers and information and technology specialists, being part of the team that protects the nation can be a rewarding career.

Despite the fact that there are many partner agencies involved in NCTC operations, it still takes a legion of on-site workers to fulfill the agency's mission. From monitoring potential terrorist threats to providing computer support, there are many jobs that need to be done and people that need to do them.

For most jobs, the path to the NCTC starts with working at the Office of the Director of National Intelligence or being a government employee with the appropriate clearance elsewhere. Jobs are listed at the ODNI website. Many jobs are for current employees only, whereas others are open to external candidates. Careers can be as varied as the jobs, but the need for quality people with a commitment to securing the nation is always present. Jobs at the NCTC fall into five main categories: production and analysis, watchlisting, program resources, information and technology, and watch officers.

Counterintelligence Production

Employees in intelligence production and analysis perform vital work and produce a broad range of products for senior **policymakers** in the intelligence community as well as those in law enforcement and ODNI. These employees also prepare and deliver briefings to senior

Words to Understand

Policymaker: Person in an organization that develops guidelines or rules for the organization.

Tradecraft: Techniques and procedures of espionage.

Watchlisting: Identifying potential or known terrorists.

President Barack Obama meets with NCTC Director Michael Leiter, center right, leadership and analysts in the secure video teleconference room at the National Counterterrorism Center in McLean, VA.

policymakers inside and outside the agency. Workers are expected to employ a wide range of methods for gathering their information, as well as independently gathering information and discovering new sources of important information.

But not just anyone is suited for these jobs. The list of skills and knowledge required for work in analysis and production is quite long and includes the following;

- Ability to research, develop, and write high-quality briefings that focus on a specific issue or key U.S. policy
- Complete knowledge of all aspects of a specific region or country, such as its political climate, history, intelligence community situation, and relationships with other countries
- Complete knowledge of the intelligence community and its **tradecraft**

- Ability to remain open-minded and change opinions when new information merits it

Additional characteristics these workers should possess are critical thinking skills, problem-solving skills, and the ability to work well with other people in a team environment.

Privacy Debates

Since 2012, when the NCTC sought to receive access to other agencies' and organizations' databases, the concern that the agency was potentially invading innocent people's privacy has been voiced, both to the NCTC and to the Department of Homeland Security. In question was the NCTC's ability to upload lists of things like families hosting foreign exchange students, flight records, and so forth. These databases obviously would hold names and other information of people who are definitely not terrorists. Some agencies that supplied these databases required the NCTC to delete any information about a nonsuspected terrorist from the database within 30 days. However, due to the length of time it took to upload and organize the data, this was not always happening. Concern was also voiced about how long the NCTC keeps information. On the NCTC side of the debate, the agency says that people who appear to be innocent over time can prove to be participants in terrorist activities. The NCTC looks for trends or patterns over time, which means it needs to keep the data for long periods of time. To provide transparency in how the agency manages its data, the NCTC has published its data use policy and several reports on data collection on its website.

Watchlisting

Watchlisting is about people. It's about properly analyzing nominations by other agencies of people who may be known or suspected terrorists and adding them to Terrorist Identities Datamart Environment (TIDE) as needed. Different agencies, such as Homeland Security, Department of State, Department of Defense, and the FBI, are typically the agencies submitting nominations. It's up to watchlisting personnel to do the thorough analysis of these nominations. Watchlisters also look for and fill gaps in the identity information of those being added to TIDE, and identify strategies for preventing future gaps.

Like the analysis and production employees, candidates for these jobs must have specialized skills and knowledge that include the following:

- Knowledge of terrorist identities analysis, databases, and watchlisting processes
- Ability to communicate both verbally and in writing
- Ability to conduct research and interviews and analyze the information
- Organizational and problem-solving skills, as well as the ability to perform under pressure

Being a Resource Specialist

People who work in the area of program resources are expected to ensure that all departments and employees in the NCTC have the resources—both human and nonhuman—that they need to succeed. They are also expected to work with leaders in the agency to help them provide documentation to justify the resources they're requesting. When the NCTC is developing a new program it's up to program resources specialists to advise them of the impact these programs will have on agency resources, or to help them prepare requests for additional resources.

It takes special skills to effectively and efficiently provide this kind of critical service, including, but not limited to, the following:

- Extensive knowledge of the U.S. government budget cycle
- Ability to use analytical and critical thinking skills
- Ability to coordinate program and resource priorities
- Ability to communicate clearly and effectively

IT Leadership and Guidance

Information technology (IT) is the lifeblood of the NCTC, since most of its work involves using multiple databases and platforms for combining and searching those databases. Additionally, computers are used in just about every facet of business today. Providing IT leadership and guidance, therefore, is an important job at the NCTC.

Leadership is exactly what the NCTC is looking for in employees in this field. Employees serve primarily as project managers, assessing IT project requirements, risks, benefits, budgets, and the like. IT leaders are also expected to oversee those working on the projects and to lead contract management efforts of outside contactors.

Because of these many leadership responsibilities, IT professionals need to have excellent leadership skills. They also need the following:

- Analytical skills
- Critical thinking skills
- Expertise in managing projects
- Superior organizational, interpersonal, and problem-solving skills
- Ability to communicate clearly

Situational Awareness: Watchlisting

Like watchlisting personnel, watch officers analyze intelligence reports and maintain and communicate current situational awareness of potential terrorist situations. The main difference between watchlisters and watch officers is that watchlisters focus on specific people—known and suspected terrorists—while watch officers monitor intelligence and reports about potential terrorist threats or situations. Other responsibilities of watch officers include sharing information with internal and external stakeholders, developing and drafting briefings, and developing situational awareness products, such as reports and articles.

All of these responsibilities mean that being able to provide clear and effective communications is of the utmost importance. In addition, watch officers should possess these skills or qualities:

- Knowledge of intelligence analysis and production
- Ability to quickly assess and act when time-sensitive issues arise
- Ability to work long shifts (12.5 hours)
- Ability to work both independently and as part of a team

An intelligence bulletin issued by the FBI's Counterterrorism Division in late May 2016 warned that so-called "militia extremists" in the United States were likely to begin targeting Muslim institutions, including mosques and other religious facilities.

Old Cold War Enemy

Former KGB officer Sergei Ivanov meets with former CIA Director Robert Gates.

The Komitet Gosudarstvennoi Bezopasnosti, or KGB (you can see why the initials were used), was an extremely powerful organization in the Soviet era. But it became defunct when Communism and the Soviet Union collapsed.

To operate its spy network worldwide, it had its own organization, the PGU—the Russian abbreviation for First Chief Directorate. Both organizations were replaced in 1991 after the collapse of Communism. The KGB became the Russian Federal Security Service—abbreviated to FSB in Russian. Vladimir Putin was head of the FSB from July 25, 1998, until August 9, 1999, before becoming Russia's president.

The PGU was renamed the Foreign Intelligence Service (SVR), which has a "Directorate T" in charge of counterterrorism. It established an Antiterrorist Center in 1995 to conduct these activities, and its main unit is called Banner.

The next year saw 420 terrorist alerts. Many were bombs planted by Islamic terrorists and fighters from Chechnya, a region in the Caucasus Mountains seeking independence. Russian troops, including the FSB's active unit named Alpha, invaded Chechnya in 1994 and left in 1997 after claiming victory.

In 2006, the FSB created an Anti-Terrorist Committee whose job was to oversee and report on all anti-terrorist efforts. Since then, the committee has reported several operations. In many of them, the killing of militants has been reported.

The rise and fall of the KGB in America.

Joint Duty

If you're not sure whether you'd like to be part of the NCTC or would like to fight terrorism through one of its partner agencies, you may be able to do both. With joint duty, people who are with NCTC partner agencies can apply for joint duty assignments, working for both agencies. When the ODNI was created by the Intelligence Reform and Terrorism Prevention Act of 2004, joint duty as a means to promotions was also introduced. According to the NCTC, the act specifically says that service in more than one element of the intelligence community can be a requirement for promotion. This encourages many people to apply for joint duty. Joint duty also gives the NCTC the opportunity to train more people on antiterrorist measures.

Existing ODNI employees are encouraged to apply for one of these joint duty assignments. Those awarded an assignment travel to their new job for a specified period of time, usually one year, after which time they return to their previous job. This allows NCTC to ensure it has hired the most knowledgeable workers for the job. And workers are able to use the experience and training on the job or to obtain a more permanent job with the NCTC.

Text-Dependent Questions

1. What agency must most people work for before joining the NCTC?
2. What do counterintelligence production employees do?
3. What is the main difference between watchlisting employees and watch officers?

Research Projects

1. How does the NCTC ensure citizens' privacy? What criteria are used to ensure people aren't added to TIDE incorrectly?
2. What kind of technologies do IT professionals need knowledge of to become IT professionals at the NCTC?

CHAPTER 5

TECHNOLOGY DRIVEN

A Department of Homeland Security program manager works with a Remotec Andros bomb-disposal robot.

Today, it can be argued that nothing is more vital to protecting our nation from terrorist attacks than technologies. Without many technologies being used today, the National Counterterrorism Center (NCTC) would not have the capabilities of assessing and disseminating potential threats to the United States and other countries.

Technology has changed the world, and that holds true for the intelligence community (IC) and the NCTC. Not only are law enforcement agencies using new technologies to combat terrorism, but, unfortunately, terrorists are also using new technologies in their attacks. That is one of the biggest reasons the IC continues to invest in new technologies.

For years, terrorist organizations like ISIS have been "meeting" publicly on social media sites, such as Facebook and Twitter. But since these organizations have learned that the IC can intercept cellular phone communications, such as calls and texts, they have "gone dark," having learned to use special applications that allow them to communicate without the information being captured by IC.

According to a news report published by CNN on November 24, 2015, titled "Technology and the Fight against Terrorism," ISIS is now **encrypting** its communications using a technology called Telegram.

The IC is caught in the proverbial area "between a rock and a hard place." To allow it to undermine encryption would also mean invading the privacy of private citizens whose texts and emails might also be read by the government. It is a very fine line for the IC to walk—to sort through millions of texts and emails for those that provide the kind of information it needs, while not infringing on the privacy of law-abiding, nonterrorist citizens.

Words to Understand

Encrypting: Encoding data to protect it.

Cybercrime: Crime that occurs on the Web.

Connectivity: Communication between computers.

NATO and Cybersecurity

The North Atlantic Treaty Organization, or NATO, is the intergovernmental military alliance based on the North Atlantic Treaty, which was signed on April 4, 1949. It is another organization that is working to prevent cyberattacks or the use of technology in what it calls hybrid warfare, using cyberattacks as well as other physical weapons in an attack.

The NATO Parliamentary Assembly, an intergovernmental organization of NATO and associate countries' elected representatives, meets in London.

In July 2016, NATO officially recognized the Web as another "space," such as land, sea, or air, that must be protected. And in February 2016, it signed a technical arrangement with the European Union to work together for cyber defense. NATO also partners with private corporations to enhance its technologies and says it is committed to information sharing with other agencies.

TIDE and Its Importance

Perhaps the most important technological tool in use at the NCTC today is its Terrorist Identities Datamart Environment (TIDE). This databank contains both classified and unclassified information on people who are known or suspected to be

- terrorists; or
- aiding terrorists; or
- helping terrorists make plans and preparations.

The IC can access TIDE through a "read only" website. The NCTC offers a list of activities that lead to inclusion in the TIDE database, including the following:

- Committing international terrorist activities
- Preparing or planning international terrorist activities
- Gathering information on potential international terrorist attack targets
- Trying to raise funds for known international terrorists
- Trying to gain membership in a known international terrorist organization
- Being a member of an international terrorist organization

The information in TIDE is used to screen travelers, applications for visas, and refugee applications, and for homeland security in general. As of June 2016, there were about 1.5 million people in the TIDE database.

Johnny Michael Spann

Known to his friends as Mike, Johnny Spann was a friendly and kind young man. Popular for his dry sense of humor, great energy, and willingness to help others, he was also religious—his Church of Christ minister said, "His first priority in his life was to make sure he was right with God."

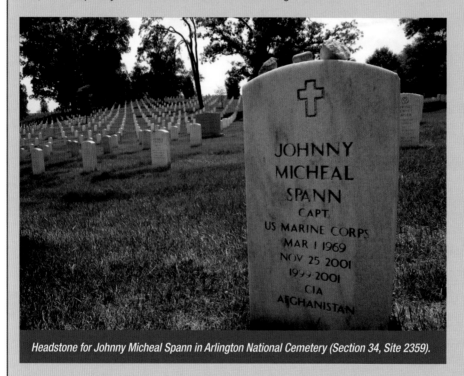

Headstone for Johnny Micheal Spann in Arlington National Cemetery (Section 34, Site 2359).

Spann grew up in the small town of Winfield, AL, where he played high school football. Graduating in 1987, he went on to earn a bachelor's degree from Auburn University and joined the Marines in 1992 for seven years, becoming a helicopter pilot. He was a captain when he left in 1999 for the Central Intelligence Agency (CIA), which he had always dreamed of joining.

Spann was killed at the age of 32, leaving a wife and three children. He was buried in Arlington National Cemetery outside Washington, DC. This cemetery holds the graves of more than 160,000 soldiers and others who have served their country, including President John F. Kennedy. The CIA director said Spann died where he wanted to be, "on the front lines serving his country," and he promised to continue "the mission Mike Spann held sacred. . . . We owe that to Mike and to every man and woman who dreams of a future free of the menace of terrorism." One of the prisoners Spann had interviewed that morning was John Walker Lindh, the American who had become a Muslim and gone to Afghanistan to fight with the Taliban. Lindh was sentenced to 20 years in prison for his terrorist activities.

Cyberattacks and the CTIIC

No one in the U.S. government, from the president to field officers of the Federal Bureau of Investigation (FBI), has any doubt that cyberattacks are the wave of the future for terrorists. Most developed nations, which are usually at the top of the list of targets for terrorists, have come to rely on the Internet to conduct business as usual. Bringing down the Internet or launching cyberattacks that prevent bigger businesses from doing business on the Internet could have significant negative impacts, not just on the businesses but on the nation's economy.

Although the government has received threats about major cyberattacks that would occur, few attacks have been credited to any international terrorist organization. One threat that has caused some concern is that ISIS hackers are working to hack into the U.S. power grid and bring it down.

According to Andre McGregor, a former FBI agent now with Tanium, a company that provides endpoint protection, one example of a terrorist cyberattack occurred when an Iranian group called Izz ad-Din al-Qassam locked out Wells Fargo customers from their accounts in an attack called a distributed denial of service attack. JP Morgan and Bank of America accounts have also been attacked in the past. The attack on Wells Fargo occurred in September 2012.

Governments don't understand cyber warfare. We need hackers.

Robert Anderson Jr., executive assistant director, criminal, cyber, response, and services branch of the FBI, addressed the Senate Committee on Homeland Security and Government Affairs in September 2014. In his address, he noted that FBI agents, analysts, and computer scientists use technical capabilities and traditional investigative techniques, including wiretaps, surveillance, and forensics, to fight **cybercrime**. He said that the FBI works side by side with federal, state, and local partners on Cyber Task Forces in each of its 56 field offices and at the National Cyber Investigative Joint Task Force (NCIJTF). The FBI also has its 24-hour cyber command center it calls CyWatch, where the agency combines the resources of the FBI and NCIJTF, allowing agents to provide **connectivity** to federal cyber centers, government agencies, FBI field offices and legal attachés, and the private sector in the event of a significant cyber intrusion. Then, in February 2015, President Obama directed the Office of the Director of National Intelligence (ODNI) to create an organization equivalent to the NCTC that would focus solely on cyberattacks. The result is the Cyber Threat Intelligence Integration Center, which supports the National Cybersecurity and Communications Integration Center, the National Cyber Investigative Joint Task Force, U.S. Cyber Command, and other relevant U.S. government entities by providing access to intelligence necessary to carry out their respective missions.

The Silk Road on the Dark Web

Remember reading about the Silk Road in history books? It was one of the first roads in history that brought about trade among many ancient civilizations, such as China. Today, the Silk Road is a part of the dark web that offers black market trade—crystal meth, weapons, explosives, lock picks, and gold bars are just a few of the items available.

The dark web and Silk Road are accessed through an anonymous network called Tor. If a person were to try to access a specific dark website through Tor, the request would be bounced randomly through volunteer computers called nodes before leaving Tor and arriving at the target site. This makes their online movements much more difficult to track. Tor can be used to access sites on the regular Web, but servers are often assigned special addresses that can only be reached within the Tor network. These hidden services are what most people think of when they hear the term dark web. Tor is probably the most well-known and well-established program used to access the dark web.

Despite the fact that Tor was originally developed by the U.S. Department of Defense, it is now a volunteer-run nonprofit operation. According to Tor volunteer operators, it is used every day for a wide variety of purposes by normal people, the military, journalists, law enforcement officers, activists, and many others. But its most famous use is for accessing the dark web.

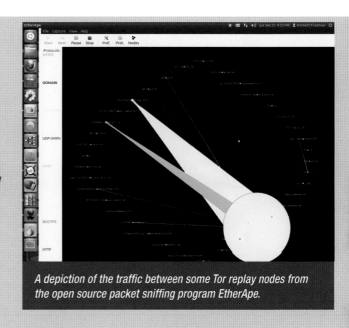

A depiction of the traffic between some Tor replay nodes from the open source packet sniffing program EtherApe.

Text-Dependent Questions

1. What is TIDE?
2. What is Tor?
3. What is CyWatch?

Research Projects

1. What are the legal and beneficial uses of Tor and who uses Tor in these ways?
2. How many people work for the Cyber Threat Intelligence Integration Center, and how do those interested in working there apply?

The first rule for first responders: be ready to respond!

T hanks to the National Counterterrorism Center's (NCTC's) Joint Counterterrorism Assessment Team (JCAT), first responders and public safety officials from around the nation can work side by side with NCTC professionals, helping to assess and communicate terrorist intelligence to the public and other safety professionals.

After September 11, it became clear that first responders across the nation needed to be just as informed, trained, and prepared for terrorist attacks as those in government channels and the intelligence community. As part of the NCTC mission and government mandate, the JCAT was organized. Now state, local, **tribal**, and territorial first responders and public safety professionals from around the country have the opportunity to work side by side with federal intelligence analysts from the NCTC, as well as the Department of Homeland Security and the Federal Bureau of Investigation. This team researches, produces, and **disseminates** counterterrorism intelligence to the public and government officials.

Local Law Enforcement and Terrorism

San Diego, according to Federal Bureau of Investigation (FBI) agents there, is a region that has been a throughway for a number of terror figures over the years. Because of this, a special task force was assembled, composed of about 75 special agents, officers, and analysts. Called the Joint Terrorism Task Force, its members come from every level of government agency—local, state, and federal.

Because of the increased terrorism threat across the country, agencies have agreed to loan more officers to help with the task force. The force cultivates intelligence and then feeds it to other task forces as well as the NCTC.

continued on page 64

Words to Understand

Disseminate: Disperse throughout.

Tribal: Of or relating to a tribe.

Vulnerability: The state of being defenseless against injury.

What the intelligence community has learned since September 11 is that first responders at every level need to be trained and informed, rather than shut out due to the fear they will compromise sensitive intelligence. After the attack in San Bernardino, CA, in which two terrorists killed 14 people and injured 22 others, the San Diego task force has met to identify potential areas of vulnerability. The attack, that took place on December 2, 2015, was conducted by Syed Rizwan Farook and Tashfeen Malik at the Inland Regional Center where Farook was an employee. The organization was holding its holiday party when the attack took place.

The shooters' Ford Expedition SUV, involved in the shootout.

The task force is also being assisted by about 2,800 terror liaison officers working at police agencies across the county. They have been trained to handle terror-related tips they receive and to help other local law enforcement agencies respond.

Products by JCAT

While working with NCTC and other agencies, JCAT works to develop and publish specific products and resources for first responders and law enforcement organizations across the nation. Most of these products are not available to the general public, and those seeking to read them must have the proper credentials to access them. Others, including most of the resources, are online and available. Classified products are accessed only on the following websites:

- Law Enforcement Online via the JCAT Special Interest Group (SIG)
- Homeland Security Information Network via the JCAT tab on the Emergency Services Community of Interest
- Domestic Security Alliance Council Website

The products include the following:

- Intelligence Guide for First Responders, which describes how first responders should process and react to intelligence about potential terrorists and terrorist operations
- Roll Call Release, which highlights potential targets, preattack indicators, and terrorism-related events for state, local, tribal, territorial, and private sector public safety and security personnel
- First Responder Toolbox, an ad hoc reference aid intended to promote counterterrorism coordination among federal, state, local, tribal, and territorial government authorities and partnerships with private sector officials in deterring, preventing, disrupting, and responding to terrorist attacks

JCAT

JOINT COUNTERTERRORISM ASSESSMENT TEAM

INTELLIGENCE GUIDE
FOR FIRST RESPONDERS

The JCAT 2016 Intelligence Guide for First Responders Cover Page

Joining JCAT

Becoming a member of JCAT means applying for a JCAT fellowship. The fellowship is open to public safety professionals—law enforcement, emergency medical services, fire service, intelligence, homeland security, and public health officials—from state, local, tribal, and territorial agencies (SLTT). JCAT fellows must commit to working on the team for one year in Washington, DC. Fellows do not receive a salary or similar monies from the JCAT agency that sponsors them. They continue to receive their usual salary from their home agency. The sponsoring agency does pay travel expenses, housing, local transportation, and so forth. The Public safety professionals interested in a JCAT fellowship go through a 9- to 16-month application and

The Journal of
COUNTER
Since 1986
TERRORISM
& Homeland Security International

Women Are The
"Biggest Losers" In The Arab Spring

The Most Credible Source of Terrorism Information in Print Today

Keep On Sale Until May 21, 2014

Terrorism Trends & Forecasts 2014

If Iraq Falls, Is Nuclear War Inevitable?

The Terrorist Threats Against Canada
And Its Counterterrorism Response

Law Enforcement's Higher Calling
In The Time Of The NSA

In The Desert:
SEAL Team SIX And The Rescue Of
Aid Worker Jessica Buchanan

An IACSP Interview With
Sandra V. Grimes, Former CIA Officer

CELEBRATING
28 YEARS
IN PRINT

Spring Issue
Vol. 20, No. 1, 2014
Printed in the U.S.A.
IACSP.COM

$5.99US $7.99CAN

4 1>

0 71486 01835 3

POLICE

PC

IACSP

Veneratio Diligentia Vires

Seeking the Edge Through Education, Training, and Technology

Counterterrorism magazine.

U.S. Park Police SWAT team members take part in a hostage-crisis training exercise in which the "terrorists" have chemical and biological agents.

screening process. At the end of the process, if chosen for a fellowship, the professional gains top secret government clearance. In addition, fellows gain critical experience and knowledge related to assessing and addressing terrorist threats and tips. They also get deep insights into the process used by the intelligence community and the experience of networking with other counterterrorist professionals.

So what is JCAT looking for in a fellow? First responder training is highly desirable, as well as experience in one of the following areas: law enforcement, fire service, multiagency task forces, long-term investigations, public safety, public health, intelligence, critical infrastructure, or information sharing/homeland security. If you don't have experience in one of those fields but you conduct research and analysis to produce intelligence assessments for the SLTT community; interpret investigative information and extrapolate data for analysis, evaluation, and dissemination to appropriate officials; and identify trends and knowledge gaps relating to terrorist plans, intentions, and capabilities for the SLTT community, you also qualify to apply.

Text-Dependent Questions

1. What does JCAT stand for?
2. Name one product JCAT produces.
3. What is Roll Call Release?

Research Projects

1. How many fellowships are offered altogether and which sponsoring agencies sponsor the most fellows?
2. How many people completed a JCAT fellowship?

Series Glosssary

Air marshal: Armed guard traveling on an aircraft to protect the passengers and crew; the air marshal is often disguised as a passenger.

Annexation: To incorporate a country or other territory within the domain of a state.

Armory: A supply of arms for defense or attack.

Assassinate: To murder by sudden or secret attack, usually for impersonal reasons.

Ballistic: Of or relating to firearms.

Biological warfare: Also known as germ warfare, this is war fought with biotoxins—harmful bacteria or viruses that are artificially propagated and deliberately dispersed to spread sickness among an enemy.

Cartel: A combination of groups with a common action or goal.

Chemical warfare: The use of poisonous or corrosive substances to kill or incapacitate the enemy; it differs from biological warfare in that the chemicals concerned are not organic, living germs.

Cold War: A long and bitter enmity between the United States and the Free World and the Soviet Union and its Communist satellites, which went on from 1945 to the collapse of Communism in 1989.

Communism: A system of government in which a single authoritarian party controls state-owned means of production.

Conscription: Compulsory enrollment of persons especially for military service.

Consignment: A shipment of goods or weapons.

Contingency operations: Operations of a short duration and most often performed at short notice, such as dropping supplies into a combat zone.

Counterintelligence: Activities designed to collect information about enemy espionage and then to thwart it.

Covert operations: Secret plans and activities carried out by spies and their agencies.

Cyberterrorism: A form of terrorism that seeks to cause disruption by interfering with computer networks.

Democracy: A government elected to rule by the majority of a country's people.

Depleted uranium: One of the hardest known substances, it has most of its radioactivity removed before being used to make bullets.

Dissident: A person who disagrees with an established religious or political system, organization, or belief.

Embargo: A legal prohibition on commerce.

Emigration: To leave one country to move to another country.

Extortion: The act of obtaining money or other property from a person by means of force or intimidation.

Extradite: To surrender an alleged criminal from one state or nation to another having jurisdiction to try the charge.

Federalize/federalization: The process by which National Guard units, under state command in normal circumstances, are called up by the president in times of crisis to serve the federal government of the United States as a whole.

Genocide: The deliberate and systematic destruction of a racial, political, or cultural group.

Guerrilla: A person who engages in irregular warfare, especially as a member of an independent unit carrying out harassment and sabotage.

Hijack: To take unlawful control of a ship, train, aircraft, or other form of transport.

Immigration: The movement of a person or people ("immigrants") into a country; as opposed to emigration, their movement out.

Indict: To charge with a crime by the finding or presentment of a jury (as a grand jury) in due form of law.

Infiltrate: To penetrate an organization, like a terrorist network.

Infrastructure: The crucial networks of a nation, such as transportation and communication, and also including government organizations, factories, and schools.

Insertion: Getting into a place where hostages are being held.

Insurgent: A person who revolts against civil authority or an established government.

Internment: To hold someone, especially an immigrant, while his or her application for residence is being processed.

Logistics: The aspect of military science dealing with the procurement, maintenance, and transportation of military matériel, facilities, and personnel.

Matériel: Equipment, apparatus, and supplies used by an organization or institution.

Militant: Having a combative or aggressive attitude.

Militia: a military force raised from civilians, which supports a regular army in times of war.

Narcoterrorism: Outrages arranged by drug trafficking gangs to destabilize government, thus weakening law enforcement and creating conditions for the conduct of their illegal business.

NATO: North Atlantic Treaty Organization; an organization of North American and European countries formed in 1949 to protect one another against possible Soviet aggression.

Naturalization: The process by which a foreigner is officially "naturalized," or accepted as a U.S. citizen.

Nonstate actor: A terrorist who does not have official government support.

Ordnance: Military supplies, including weapons, ammunition, combat vehicles, and maintenance tools and equipment.

Refugee: A person forced to take refuge in a country not his or her own, displaced by war or political instability at home.

Rogue state: A country, such as Iraq or North Korea, that ignores the conventions and laws set by the international community; rogue states often pose a threat, either through direct military action or by harboring terrorists.

Sortie: One mission or attack by a single plane.

Sting: A plan implemented by undercover police in order to trap criminals.

Surveillance: To closely watch over and monitor situations; the USAF employs many different kinds of surveillance equipment and techniques in its role as an intelligence gatherer.

Truce: A suspension of fighting by agreement of opposing forces.

UN: United Nations; an international organization, of which the United States is a member, that was established in 1945 to promote international peace and security.

Chronology

1941: July 11, President Franklin D. Roosevelt establishes the office of Coordinator of Information (COI), the model for the CIA.

1942: June 13, the COI becomes the Office of Strategic Services (OSS).

1945: October 1, the OSS is disbanded.

1946: January 22, President Harry S. Truman's directive establishes the Central Intelligence Group (CIG).

1947: July 26, the National Security Act of 1947 comes into effect, creating the independent CIA to replace the CIG; Rear Admiral Roscoe H. Hillenkoetter is the first director.

1949: The Central Intelligence Act of 1949 gives Congress authority to regulate the CIA.

1953: February 26, Allen Dulles becomes CIA director and serves until November 29, 1961.

1960: May 5, the Soviet Union downs a CIA U2 spy plane; the pilot, Gary Powers, survives and is exchanged for a Soviet spy in 1962.

1961: CIA-supported Cuban refugees invade Cuba at the Bay of Pigs and are defeated.

1962: October 14, a CIA U2 plane discovers Soviet missile sites in Cuba.

1976: January 30, former president George H. W. Bush becomes CIA director and serves until January 20, 1977.

1986: The CIA's Counterterrorist Center (CTC) is established by CIA director William Casey.

1988: December 21, Libyan terrorists bomb Pan American Flight 103 over Lockerbie, Scotland, killing 270; the CIA is placed in charge of the investigation.

1997: July 10, George J. Tenet is named CIA director.

1998: August 7, Islamic extremists bomb the U.S. embassies in Kenya and Tanzania; the CIA and FBI work together to track the terrorists.

2000: October 12, the USS *Cole* is bombed off Yemen, killing 17; the CIA leads the investigation.

2001: September 11, Islamic terrorists hijack four airliners; they fly two into the twin towers of the World Trade Center, destroying them, and one into a section of the Pentagon, causing a total of more than 3,000 deaths; the FBI and CIA link the attacks to Osama bin Laden and his Al Qaeda terrorist network.

2002: Director George J. Tenet attends talks with Palestinian Cabinet ministers in an attempt to begin the peace process in the West Bank of Israel.

2004: NCTC is formed as part of the Intelligence Reform and Terrorism Prevention Act of 2004.

2014: Nicholas Rasmussen is named director of NCTC.

Further Resources

Websites

The CIA: www.cia.gov; www.cia.gov/cia/ciakids/index.html

The FBI: www.fbi.gov

The National Intelligence Council: www.cia.gov/nic/index.htm

The Department of Defense: www.defenselink.mil/pubs/dod101

The NCTC: www.nctc.gov

The Defense Intelligence Agency: www.dia.mil

Further Reading

Baer, Robert. *See No Evil: The True Story of a Ground Soldier in the CIA's War on Terrorism.* New York: Crown Publishing, 2002.

Colarik, Andrew. *Cyber Terrorism: Political and Economic Implications.* Hershey, PA: IGI Global, 2006.

Hamilton, John. *Operation Noble Eagle: The War on Terrorism.* Minneapolis: Abdo & Daughters, 2002.

January, Brendan. *The CIA.* Danbury, CT: Franklin Watts, 2002.

Kaplan, Fred. *Dark Territory: The Secret History of Cyber War.* New York: Simon & Schuster, 2016.

Landau, Elaine. *Osama bin Laden: A War against the West.* New York: Twenty-First Century Books, 2002.

Louis, Nancy. *Osama bin Laden.* Minneapolis: Abdo & Daughters, 2002.

Melton, H. Keith. *The Ultimate Spy Book.* New York: DK Publishing, 1996.

Platt, Richard. *Eyewitness: Spy.* New York: DK Publishing, 2000.

Prados, John. *America Confronts Terrorism: Understanding the Danger and How to Think about It.* Chicago: Ivan R. Dee, 2002.

Smith, Dennis. *Report from Ground Zero: The Story of the Rescue Efforts at the World Trade Center.* New York: Viking Press, 2002.

Index

Afghanistan 38, 56
airport; security 23, 28–29
Al Qaeda 21, 24, 28, 38, 75

bin Laden, Osama 24, 28, 38–40, 75
   Al Qaeda 28, 38, 75
   CIA operations 28, 40, 75
   FBI operations 75
Britain; Special Operations Executive (SOE) 10
Bush, George W. 38, 74

Casey, William, Director, CIA 74
Central Intelligence Agency (CIA) 9–15, 17–18,
   28, 31, 33, 38, 40, 50, 56, 74–75
counterterrorism operations 9, 25, 36–37, 50
Cold War 12, 50, 71
computer systems, vulnerability 27, 31, 60, 71
counterterrorism *see also* terrorism 9, 11, 15,
   17–18, 23–25, 27, 30, 33, 36–37, 43–44,
   49–50–51, 53, 56, 63, 65, 67, 71, 75
   Al Qaeda 24
   CIA role 15, 33
   FBI role 15
   foreign agencies 36
   government bodies 36
   interagency cooperation 15, 17, 25, 33, 35–37
Counterterrorist Center (CTC) 74
Cuba 14, 74

Defense Intelligence Agency (DIA) 18
Department of Homeland Security (DHS) 17–18,
   36, 45, 52, 63, 66
Donovan, Major General William J. 9, 11–13
Dulles, Allen, Director, CIA 74

equipment, intelligence-gathering 31

Federal Bureau of Investigation (FBI) 9, 15,
   17–18, 28, 33, 36–37, 45, 49, 57, 60, 63,
   74–75
   CIA, liaising 15, 17, 28, 74
   counterterrorism role 17, 28, 33, 49, 63

   criticized 28
   Oklahoma City bombing 37

Hall, Virginia 13

intelligence gathering 9, 28, 38, 44, 73
   aerial reconnaissance 40
   electronic information 6, 36
   equipment 31
   foreign agencies 11
interagency liaison, counterterrorism 64
Iraq 24, 38, 73
Islamic terrorism 21, 38, 50, 74

Joint Chiefs of Staff 9–11

McVeigh, Timothy 20, 37

National Counterterrorism Center (NCTC) 9, 11,
   15–18, 23–29, 31, 33, 35–37, 42–47, 51,
   53, 55, 60, 63, 65–66, 75
   early history 9, 15
   external scrutiny 45
   FBI, liaising 17–18
   foreign agencies, liaising 17–18, 25, 28, 33
   founded 15
   operations 25, 36–37, 43
   structure 16–17
National Security Council 25

Office of Strategic Services (OSS) 10–11, 74
Oklahoma City bombing 20, 37

Pentagon building, Washington, DC 21, 31, 74
Putin, Vladimir 50

Roosevelt, Franklin D. 8–9, 74
Russia, security services 14, 50

September 11, 2001 9, 15, 19, 21, 28, 33, 37–38,
   63–64
   CIA operations 15, 28

Spann, Johnny Michael 56

Taliban 38, 56
    Afghan government 38
    prisoners 56
Tenet, George J., Director, CIA 28, 74
terrorism *see also* counterterrorism; September
        11, 2001 9, 11, 15, 17–19, 21, 23–25,
        27–28, 30, 33, 36–38, 43–44, 49–50–51,
        53, 56, 63–65, 67, 71, 75
    cyberattacks 27, 29, 31, 54, 57, 60
    Islamic 21, 24, 50, 74

organizations 24, 28, 31, 53, 55, 57
    weapons of mass destruction (WMD) 33–34
Transportation Security Administration (TSA) 26,
    28–29
Truman, Harry S. 11, 74

U-2 spy plane 14

weapons of mass destruction (WMD) 33–34
World Trade Center, New York 16, 21, 74
World War II 9, 13

A New York City Police Department counterterrorism officer watches over the crowd in Times Square in front of a giant illuminate American flag.

About the Author

Kelly Kagamas Tomkies is a writer and editor with nearly 20 years of experience. Her published works include books and articles, as well as educational content for textbooks and publishers. She lives in Columbus, OH, with her husband, Kevin, and her son, Duncan, two dogs, a cat, and an African clawed frog.

About the Consultant

Manny Gomez, an expert on terrorism and security, is President of MG Security Services and a former Principal Relief Supervisor and Special Agent with the FBI. He investigated terrorism and espionage cases as an agent in the National Security Division. He was a certified undercover agent and successfully completed Agent Survival School. Chairman of the Board of the National Law Enforcement Association (NLEA), Manny is also a former Sergeant in the New York Police Department (NYPD) where he supervised patrol and investigative activities of numerous police officers, detectives and civilian personnel. Mr. Gomez worked as a uniformed and plainclothes officer in combating narcotics trafficking, violent crimes, and quality of life concerns. He has executed over 100 arrests and received Departmental recognition on eight separate occasions. Mr. Gomez has a Bachelor's Degree and Master's Degree and is a graduate of Fordham University School of Law where he was on the Dean's list. He is admitted to the New York and New Jersey Bar. He served honorably in the United States Marine Corps infantry.